PACHYCEPHALOSAURUS

Titles in the Dinosaur Profiles series include:

DINOSAUR PROFILES

PACHYCEPHALOSAURUS

Text by Fabio Marco Dalla Vecchia
Illustrations by Leonello Calvetti and Luca Massini

BLACKBIRCH PRESS
An imprint of Thomson Gale, a part of The Thomson Corporation

THOMSON

GALE

Detroit • New York • San Francisco • New Haven, Conn. • Waterville, Maine • London

THOMSON
GALE

Computer illustrations 3D and 2D: Leonello Calvetti and Luca Massini

Photographs: page 20, Ballista/English Wikipedia; page 21, Richard T. Nowitz/CORBIS

LIBRARY OF CONGRESS CATALOGING-IN-PUBLICATION DATA

Dalla Vecchia, Fabio Marco.
Pachycephalosaurus / text by Fabio Marco Dalla Vecchia ; Illustrations by Leonello Calvetti and Luca Massini.
    p. cm.—(Dinosaur profiles)
Includes bibliographical references and index.
ISBN-13: 978-1-4103-0741-5 (hardcover)
ISBN-10: 1-4103-0741-7 (hardcover)
1. Pachycephalosaurus—Juvenile literature. 2. Dinosaurs—Evolution—Juvenile literature. I. Calvetti, Leonello, ill. II. Massini, Luca, ill. III. Title.

QE862.O65D365 2007
567.914—dc22
                                                        2006103379

Contents

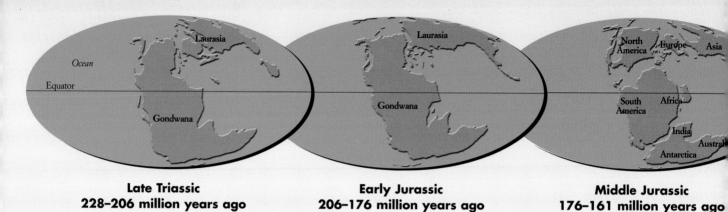

Late Triassic
228–206 million years ago

Early Jurassic
206–176 million years ago

Middle Jurassic
176–161 million years ago

A Changing World

Earth's long history began 4.6 billion years ago. Dinosaurs are some of the most fascinating animals from the planet's long past.

The word *dinosaur* comes from the word *dinosauria*. This word was invented by the English scientist Richard Owen in 1842. It comes from two Greek words, *deinos* and *sauros*. Together, these words mean "terrifying lizard."

The dinosaur era, also called the Mesozoic era, lasted from 228 million years ago to 65 million years ago. It is divided into three periods. The first, the Triassic period, lasted about 42 million years. The second, the Jurassic period, lasted 61 million years. The third, the Cretaceous period, lasted about 79 million years. Dinosaurs ruled the world for a huge time span of 160 million years.

Like dinosaurs, mammals appeared at the end of the Triassic period. During the time of dinosaurs, mammals were small animals the size of a mouse. Only after dinosaurs became extinct did mammals develop into the many forms that exist today. Humans never met Mesozoic dinosaurs. The dinosaurs were gone nearly 65 million years before humans appeared on Earth.

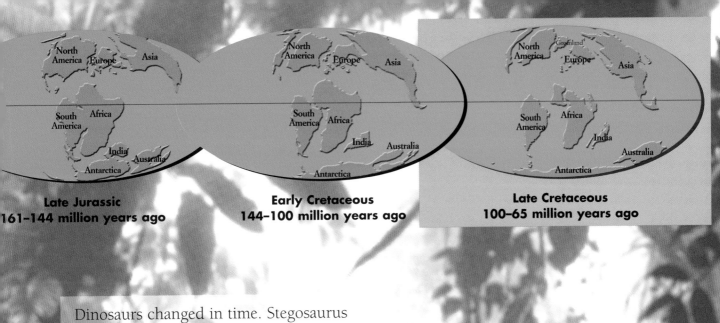

Late Jurassic
161–144 million years ago

Early Cretaceous
144–100 million years ago

Late Cretaceous
100–65 million years ago

Dinosaurs changed in time. Stegosaurus
and Brachiosaurus no longer existed
when Tyrannosaurus and Triceratops
appeared 75 million years later.

The dinosaur world was different
from today's world. The climate
was warmer, with few extremes.
The position of the continents was
different. Plants were constantly
changing, and grass did not even exist.

A Very Hard Head

The name *Pachycephalosaurus* comes from Greek and means "thick-headed lizard." The upper part of this dinosaur's skull was an amazing 9 inches (23cm) thick. It was shaped like a dome and looked something like a person's bald head. It was surrounded by bony knobs and spikes.

Only the skull of a Pachycephalosaurus has been found. Based on the size of the skull, scientists believe that Pachycephalosaurus was about 26 feet (8m) long. It probably weighed between 1 and 2 tons (0.9 and 1.8 metric tons). Experts think that Pachycephalosaurus was bipedal, meaning it moved around on its two hind limbs. It was related to the smaller Stygimoloch and Dracorex.

Pachycephalosaurus lived during the late Cretaceous Period, not long before dinosaurs became extinct 65.5 million years ago. Pachycephalosaurus remains have been discovered in what are today Wyoming, Montana, and South Dakota.

This map shows part of North America during the late Cretaceous period. The brown areas show mountains. The red dots show places where Pachycephalosaurus fossils have been discovered.

PACHYCEPHALOSAURUS BABIES

Very little is known about Pachycephalosaurus or its relatives. No Pachycephalosaurus eggs or nests have ever been found. But scientists believe that the skulls of the young dinosaurs were smoother than those of adults, with much smaller knobs and spikes.

PLANTS TO EAT

The teeth of Pachycephalosaurus were small and triangle-shaped. They also had points around the edges. This means that this dinosaur probably ate plant foods such as leaves, seeds, fruit, and buds. The young may also have eaten insects.

A New Look at an Old Idea

Paleontologists (scientists who study dinosaurs) once thought that Pachycephalosauruses fought with each other by butting heads as bighorn sheep do. Today, though, many no longer believe this idea. They think that fighting in this way would have broken these dinosaurs' necks. And one scientist who studied many skulls of Pachycephalosaurus and its relatives found no scars from old injuries. Butting heads would have caused such injuries.

Using Its Head

Although Pachycephalosauruses probably did not fight by butting heads, they might have butted each other in the side as bison do. They may also have used their domed heads to defend against predators. The bony knobs and spikes around the skull might have helped a Pachycephalosaurus attract a mate.

THE PACHYCEPHALOSAURUS BODY

The most unusual feature of Pachycephalosaurus was its head. The dome at the top of the skull was solid bone, not hollow as human skulls are. At the base of the dome were bony knobs and spikes. The snout was long and pointed, and also had cone-shaped knobs.

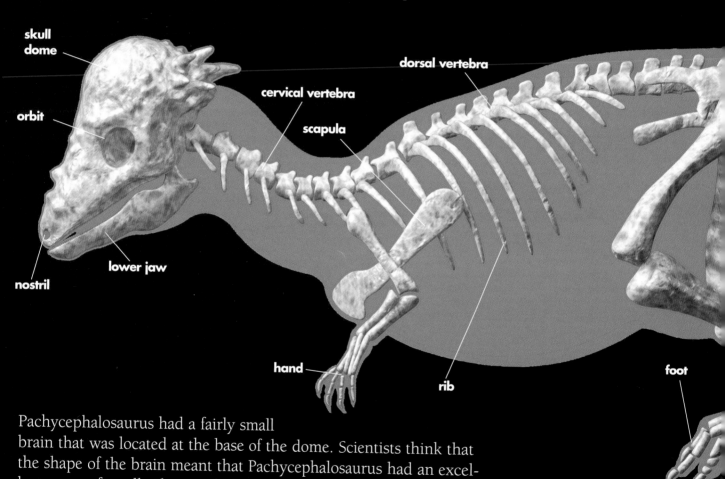

skull dome

dorsal vertebra

cervical vertebra

orbit

scapula

lower jaw

nostril

hand

rib

foot

Pachycephalosaurus had a fairly small brain that was located at the base of the dome. Scientists think that the shape of the brain meant that Pachycephalosaurus had an excellent sense of smell. This would have helped it find food and escape from predators. Scientists also believe Pachycephalosaurus had good eyesight, because the skull has very large orbits, or eye holes.

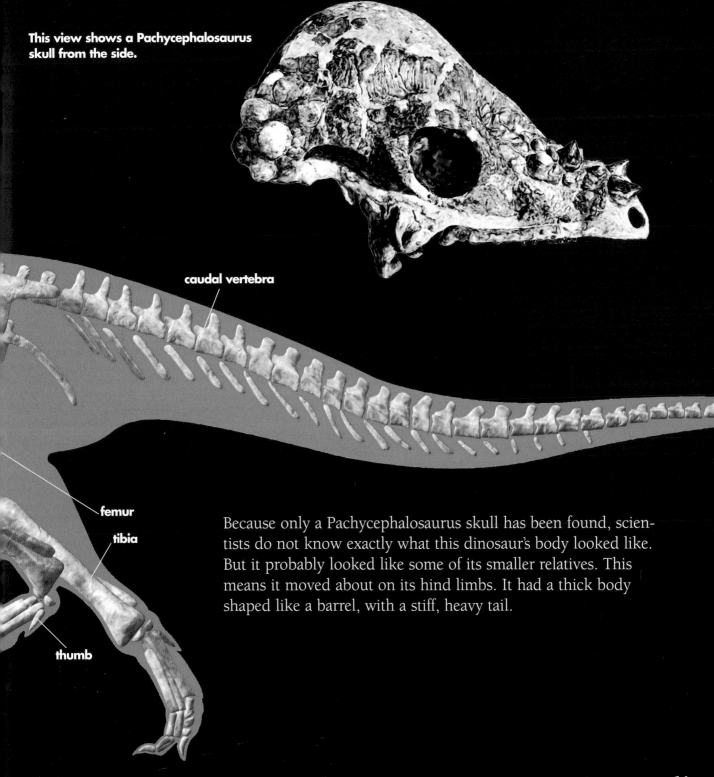

This view shows a Pachycephalosaurus skull from the side.

caudal vertebra

femur

tibia

thumb

Because only a Pachycephalosaurus skull has been found, scientists do not know exactly what this dinosaur's body looked like. But it probably looked like some of its smaller relatives. This means it moved about on its hind limbs. It had a thick body shaped like a barrel, with a stiff, heavy tail.

Digging Up Pachycephalosaurus

Pieces of Pachycephalosaurus skulls were found as early as 1860, but the first nearly complete skull was not discovered until 1940. It was found north of Ekalaka, Montana. Today, that skull is on display in the American Museum of Natural History in New York City.

At least four Pachycephalosaurus skulls, and a few bones, have been discovered since then. But no complete skeletons have yet been found.

Above: This model is of Stegoceras, a close relative of Pachycephalosaurus. It is displayed at Midland Provincial Park in Alberta, Canada.

Left: This Pachycephalosaurus skull is on display in the Oxford University Museum of Natural History in Great Britain.

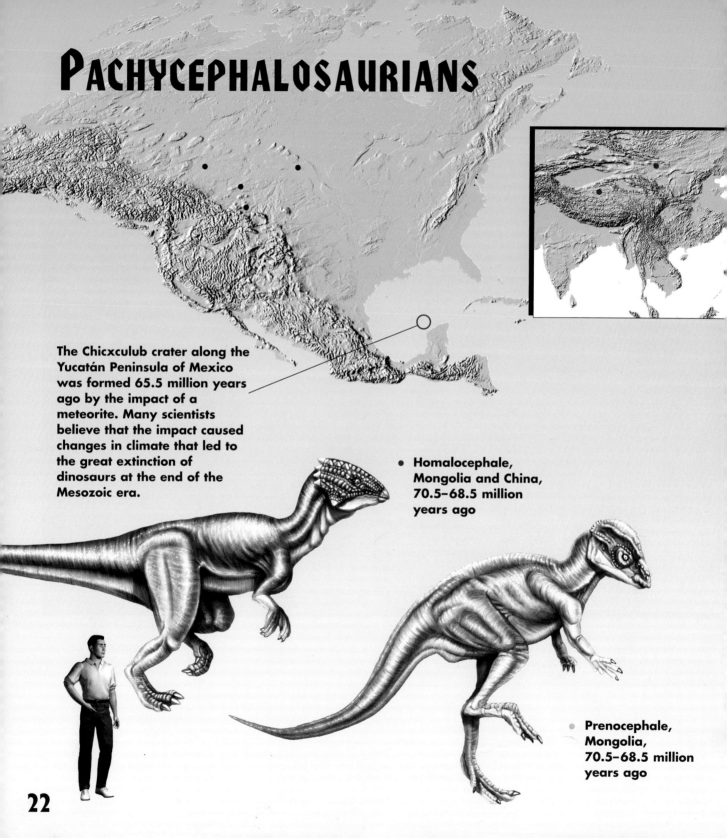

PACHYCEPHALOSAURIANS

The Chicxculub crater along the Yucatán Peninsula of Mexico was formed 65.5 million years ago by the impact of a meteorite. Many scientists believe that the impact caused changes in climate that led to the great extinction of dinosaurs at the end of the Mesozoic era.

- Homalocephale, Mongolia and China, 70.5–68.5 million years ago

- Prenocephale, Mongolia, 70.5–68.5 million years ago

The pachycephalosaurians, which include Pachycephalosaurus and its relatives, are also known as thick-headed or dome-headed dinosaurs. Homalocephale belongs to this group even though the upper part of its skull was flat.

Opposite: This map shows sites where the pachycephalosaurians pictured below have been found.

• **Stegoceras, U.S. and Canada, 76.5–75 million years ago**

• **Pachycephalosaurus, U.S. and Canada, 67–65.5 million years ago**

THE GREAT EXTINCTION

Pachycephalosaurus was one of the last dinosaurs. Sixty-five million years ago, dinosaurs became extinct. This may have happened because a large meteorite struck Earth. A wide crater caused by a meteorite 65 million years ago has been located along the coast of the Yucatán Peninsula in Mexico. The impact of the meteorite would have produced an enormous amount of dust. This dust would have stayed suspended in the atmosphere and blocked sunlight for a long time. A lack of sunlight would have caused a drastic drop in Earth's temperature and killed plants. The plant-eating dinosaurs would have died, starved and frozen. As a result, meat-eating dinosaurs would have had no prey and would also have starved.

Some scientists believe dinosaurs did not die out completely. They think that birds were feathered dinosaurs that survived the great extinction. That would make the present-day chicken and all of its feathered relatives descendants of the large dinosaurs.

THE EVOLUTION OF DINOSAURS

The oldest dinosaur fossils are 220–225 million years old and have been found mainly in South America. They have also been found in Africa, India, and North America. Dinosaurs probably evolved from small and nimble bipedal reptiles like the Triassic Lagosuchus of Argentina. Dinosaurs were able to rule the world because their legs were held directly under the body, like those of modern mammals. This made them faster and less clumsy than other reptiles.

Since 1887, dinosaurs have been divided into two groups based on the structure of their hips. Saurischian dinosaurs had hips shaped like those of modern lizards. Ornithischian dinosaurs had hips shaped like those of modern birds.

Triceratops is one of the ornithischian dinosaurs, whose hip bones (inset) are shaped like those of modern birds.

Tyrannosaurus is in the saurischian group of dinosaurs, whose hip bones (inset) are shaped like those of modern lizards.

There are two main groups of saurischians. One group is sauropodomorphs. This group includes sauropods, such as Brachiosaurus. Sauropods ate plants and were quadrupedal, meaning they walked on four legs. The other group of saurischians, theropods, includes bipedal meat-eating predators. Some paleontologists believe birds are a branch of theropod dinosaurs.

Ornithischians are all plant eaters. They are divided into three groups. Thyreophorans include the quadrupedal stegosaurians, including Stegosaurus, and ankylosaurians, including Ankylosaurus. The other two groups are ornithopods, which includes Edmontosaurus and marginocephalians.

25

A Dinosaur's Family Tree

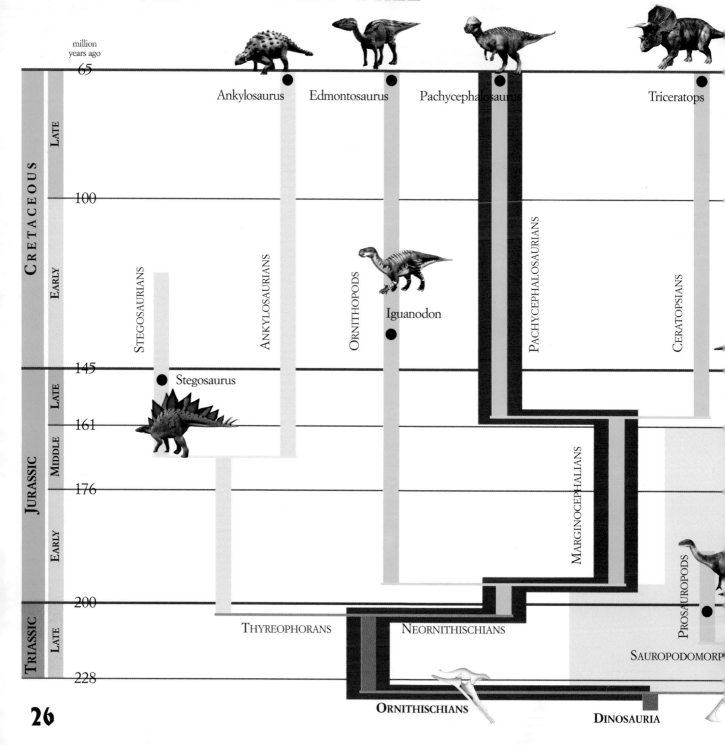

million years ago

65

100

145

161

176

200

228

CRETACEOUS

JURASSIC

TRIASSIC

LATE

EARLY

LATE

MIDDLE

EARLY

LATE

Ankylosaurus

Edmontosaurus

Pachycephalosaurus

Triceratops

STEGOSAURIANS

Stegosaurus

ANKYLOSAURIANS

ORNITHOPODS

Iguanodon

PACHYCEPHALOSAURIANS

CERATOPSIANS

MARGINOCEPHALIANS

PROSAUROPODS

THYREOPHORANS

NEORNITHISCHIANS

SAUROPODOMORP

ORNITHISCHIANS

DINOSAURIA

Giganotosaurus

Ornithomimus

Tyrannosaurus

Velociraptor

ORNITHOMIMOIDEANS

TYRANNOSAUROIDS

OVIRAPTOROSAURIANS

DEINONYCHOSAURIANS

BIRDS

Deinonychus

Scipionyx

SAUROPODS

Caudipteryx

hiosaurus Diplodocus

Ornitholestes

THEROPODS

aurus

GLOSSARY

Bipedal moving on two feet

Caudal related to the tail

Cervical related to the neck

Claws sharp, pointed nails on the fingers and toes of predators

Cretaceous period the period of geological time between 144 and 65 million years ago

Dorsal related to the back

Evolution changes in living things over time

Femur thigh bone

Fossil part of a living thing, such as a skeleton or leaf imprint, that has been preserved in Earth's crust from an earlier geological age

Jurassic period the period of geological time between 206 and 145 million years ago

Mesozoic era the period of geological time between 228 and 65 million years ago

Meteorite a piece of iron or rock that falls to Earth from space

Orbit the opening in the skull surrounding the eye

Paleontologist a scientist who studies prehistoric life

Predator an animal that hunts other animals for food

Prey an animal that is hunted by other animals for food

Quadrupedal moving on four feet

Skeleton the structure of an animal body, made up of bones

Skull the bones that form the head and face

Tibia shinbone

Triassic period the period of geological time between 248 and 206 million years ago

Vertebra a bone of the spine

For More Information

Books

Daniel Cohen, *Pachycephalosaurus*. Mankato, MN: Capstone Press, 2006.

Chris Maynard, *The Best Book of Dinosaurs*. Boston: Kingfisher, 2005.

Bill Nye and Ian G. Saunders, *Bill Nye the Science Guy's Great Big Book of Science: Featuring Oceans and Dinosaurs*. New York: Hyperion, 2005.

Web Sites

Pachycephalosaurus wyomingensis and Pterodactylus
http://www.gate.net/~mcorriss/PachPter.htm
This Web site has pictures of a Pachycephalosaurus skull and bones found in South Dakota.

Prehistoric Life
http://www.bbc.co.uk/sn/prehistoric_life/
This section of the BBC Web site contains a great deal of information about dinosaurs, including galleries of illustrations along with games and quizzes.

The Smithsonian National Museum of Natural History
http://www.nmnh.si.edu/paleo/dino/
A virtual tour of the Smithsonian's National Museum of Natural History dinosaur exhibits.

About the Author

Fabio Marco Dalla Vecchia is the curator of the Paleontological Museum of Monfalcone in Gorizia, Italy. He has participated in several paleontological field works in Italy and other countries and has directed paleontological excavations in Italy. He is the author of more than 50 scientific articles that have been published in national and international journals.

Index

INDEX